Cinco de Mayo

By Mary Dodson Wade

Consultant
Nanci R. Vargus, Ed.D.
Assistant Professor
Literacy Education
University of Indianapolis
Indianapolis, Indiana

Children's Press®
A Division of Scholastic Inc.
New York   Toronto   London   Auckland   Sydney
Mexico City   New Delhi   Hong Kong
Danbury, Connecticut

Designer: Herman Adler Design
Photo Researcher: Caroline Anderson
The photo on the cover shows a dancer at a Cinco de Mayo festival.

Library of Congress Cataloging-in-Publication Data

Wade, Mary Dodson.
  Cinco de Mayo / by Mary Dodson Wade.
     p. cm. — (Rookie read–about holidays)
  ISBN 0-516-22664-9 (lib. bdg.)   0-516-27489-9 (pbk.)
  1. Cinco de Mayo (Mexican holiday)—Juvenile literature. 2. Cinco de
Mayo, Battle of, 1862—Juvenile literature. 3. Mexico—Social life and
customs—Juvenile literature. I. Title. II. Series.
  F1233 .W33 2003
  394.26972—dc21

                                        2002015127

Cinco de Mayo!
It is time to party!

4

Parades go down the street.

Mariachi (mahr-re-AH-che) bands play music.

Dancers move their feet
to the fast music.

May 2003

Sunday	Monday	Tuesday	Wednesday	Thursday	Friday	Saturday
				1	2	3
4	**5**	6	7	8	9	10
11	12	13	14	15	16	17
18	19	20	21	22	23	24
25	26	27	28	29	30	31

Cinco de Mayo means "The Fifth of May." It celebrates something that happened in Mexico long ago.

It was 1861. The country of Mexico was free, but it had many problems.

Mexico had spent years fighting many wars. It owed a lot of money to other countries.

Many of the Mexican people were poor.

Benito Juarez (Bay-NEE-toe WHAR-ace) was president of Mexico.

He wanted to help his people. He stopped paying back money to the other countries.

11

The ruler of France wanted his money.

He also wanted to take over Mexico. He sent soldiers there.

The soldiers marched across Mexico.

General Zaragoza (SAR-ah-GO-sah) waited for the soldiers at the city of Puebla (PWAY-bla).

A hill near the city of Puebla today

He thought his men could not win the battle. The French soldiers had better weapons. They had a much bigger army, too.

General Zaragoza had
a plan. On May 5, 1862,
he put his men on two
hills outside the city.

The French tried to go up
the hills, but the Mexican
soldiers fought them off.

People act out the Battle of Puebla each year.

Then a rainstorm came.

The French soldiers
slipped in the mud.
They could not get up
the hills.

The Mexicans won
the battle!

The battle showed that Mexicans would fight hard to keep other countries from taking over Mexico.

President Juarez was proud of the soldiers. He made Cinco de Mayo a holiday.

Today, people in Mexico
and the United States
celebrate Cinco de Mayo.

Girls wear white blouses
and red and green ruffled
skirts. These are the colors
of Mexico's flag.

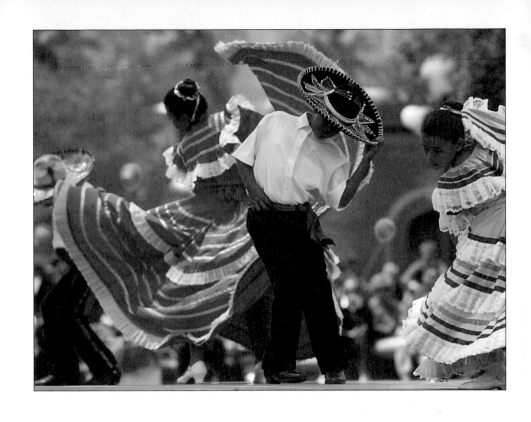

Boys wear white shirts
and red sashes. Sometimes
they wear big hats called
sombreros (som-BRAY-ros).

On Cinco de Mayo, families
go to carnivals and festivals.

They watch people
perform in shows.

Children break piñatas
(pin-YAH-tahs). Goodies
fall to the floor.

There is lots of fun
and good food.

Cinco de Mayo is a day
to remember an important
victory for Mexico.

It is a day of pride!

Words You Know

battle

carnival

festival

mariachi band

parade

piñata

president

sombrero

31

Index

About the Author

Mary Dodson Wade was an elementary teacher for twenty-five years. She has written more than thirty nonfiction books, including several in the Rookie Read-About® series. She and her husband live in Houston, Texas.

Photo Credits

Photographs © 2003: AP/Wide World Photos/Jose Luis Magana: 17, 30 top left; Art Resource, NY/Schalkwijk: 11; Bridgeman Art Library International Ltd., London/New York: 18 (Museo Nacional de Historia, Mexico City, Mexico); Dave G. Houser/HouserStock, Inc.: 6, 30 bottom right; Mary Evans Picture Library: 12; PhotoEdit: 22, 24, 30 top right (Tony Freeman), 3 (Michael Newman), 26, 31 top right (Tom Prettyman), 25, 27, 29, 30 bottom left (David Young-Wolff); The Art Archive/Picture Desk/Natural History Museum, Mexico City/Dagli Orti: 14, 15, 31 bottom left; The Image Works: cover (Kathy McLaughlin), 21 (Kent Meireis), 4, 5, 31 top left (Michael Siluk); Viesti Collection, Inc./Joe Viesti: 7, 23, 31 bottom right.